The Glow in Life

Crystal Wu

Presentation by *BookLeaf Publishing*

Web: www.bookleafpub.com

E-mail: info@bookleafpub.com

ISBN: 9789357740425

First edition 2023

I would like to dedicate my family, friends, and teachers who gave me inspiration for writing these poems. I appreciate them for being there for me and they always gave me the bright side of life.

ACKNOWLEDGEMENT

I would like to acknowledge my family were there for me always. My friends at school who made me feel like I had a place and that I can share almost anything with them. My teachers who gave me inspiration for writing these poems. They were the ones to get me through school, life, and helped me improved my writing skills. I love every single one of them for being a part of my life and I want to return the favor and share all the good in life with the readers!

PREFACE

This book is for anyone who is currently experiencing some ups and downs in life. Read this book to make yourself feel better when you are down, it really helps.

~Author

The spark in your eyes

Your eyes are like stars; they spark the divine.
Glowing bright in the night so fine,
A twinkle that takes away my pain,
of long and arduous rain.

Your eyes enliven my soul,
A sight to behold, a story to be told,
A flame that can never be tamed,
brightening the darkest day.

It is a reflection of the light of your soul,
a reminder of your inner strength and courage.
The symbol of the beauty and potential within
you,
a reminder that you can achieve anything.

It is an expression of your true self,
you are capable of greatness.

Be You

If only you would trust me.
People wear these
broken smiles :(,
trying to avoid the truth.

Looking into the mirror,
I thought about being perfect
and yet I still can't see it.
I'm afraid of never making it true

But here is raw honesty from me.
Those dreams could be farther away as forever
or as close as they can be.
It all depends

My timings is not perfect but
there is no shame in
yours and mine mistakes
We are just learning.

Nobody hates you

Nobody hates you,
Though life is sometimes cruel,
Misunderstandings come and go,
But you are loved, that's true.

You are unique, in every way,
Your worth is far beyond measure,
Take solace in that, every day,
For nobody hates you, ever.

Nobody hates you,
it's all a lie,
your life's not through,
the future's still high.

You're capable,
and most of all wise.
Achieve your goals,
your future is your prize.

You are Loved

You are loved, it is true,
no one can deny.
No matter what you do,
We will always be here for you.

You will always have a sky
full of stars, that shine.
Your heart will always contain our love
Don't listen to what they say about you

No one can make this feeling go away
You are loved more than you know.
Your life is valued, so much that,
We won't leave you, not even until the end.

I don't know how to show this,
But it is honesty coming from my heart.
Your spirit shines, a special light,
your worth is great, it is not plain to see.

Therefore, you are loved, every day
Please don't believe what they say.

Don't Change Who You Are

Be true to yourself!
Don't change your inner being!
Your heart, soul, and core remain.
Your values and beliefs will remain the same

The world will try to make you something else
But stay true to yourself
and don't change!
Who cares what others think!

Your uniqueness is what makes you special,
This is who you are
Never change yourself for someone else
It is not your fault they don't like you.

Everyone will have something bad to say
Don't let it impact who you are.
You are special for who you are!

You are Special

Your life is your choice and is a special one
Your dreams are your goals, you will surely win
your journey is your destiny
Your ideas make you unique
Your struggles teach you to strive
And your smile keeps everyone alive!

You are special and unique,
a gift so rare and true.
You share your heart and soul,
a beauty that shines through!

Your laughter is so bright and sunny,
and your courage never fades.
Your spirit is so strong
and you are the special one that was made.
:) <3 <3 <3 :)

We are not Flawless

We may not be perfect,
No one can deny,
But we are unique,
and we try to fly.

We have our flaws,
and that's just how it goes,
But it is okay to make mistakes,
We're not flawless.

We may stumble and fall,
but we can still stand tall.
Accepting our flaws
we live for the applause!

We make mistakes, it is all part of life
and should be seen as a lesson in strife.
Not perfection we seek to find,
but it is the moments of joy and peace of our
mind.

Just Try

Just try, and never give in,
Take a breath, begin again.
Start new and find that spark,
Hard work pays, no need to bark.

Just try and reach far beyond,
Push your limits, until they respond.
Your strength and courage must be set free,
once you start you will be able to feel glee.

Do not let doubts hold you back,
Let your courage be your guide!
Just try, no matter how hard
It may be, don't give up.

For what you seek, you will find
you must take the first step.
Be brave and take the chance!

Don't let fear stand in your way,
You will eventually find it to decay.

I am possible

I am possible, a dream so true,
There is a future that's within my view.
Unlock the doors, open the gates!
Unleash the power that awaits!

The sky is the limit, I can do it all,
I am possible; I will not fall.
My dreams take flight, they won't be gone,
The passion in my heart will always be a
beautiful white swan.

My journey starts with a single step
My hopes and dreams will never tire.
I will never give up, I will not accept defeat.
All I know is that I can achieve.

Failure

Failure can be hard,
It brings us disappointment,
Tho it does show us what won't work,
and that it is a perk.

Failure may be true,
but it doesn't define us.
We can still thrive and shine,
It is just a part of life.

Failure is a lesson,
a lesson we must learn.
To accept, not to repent,
unless you don't want to feel content.

It is what keeps us going,
it does not matter how.
No matter what the people throw at us,
we have to adjust!

In the end it was Failure who makes us feel
complete
and is the path we must all greet.

A Difference I can Make

I can make a difference,
Tho I know how small it may be.
The size does not matter
As long as it makes them filled with glee.

I can bring a smile to someone's face,
And spread positivity, every day!
I can be the light,
And do many good deeds.

I don't care how long I take to make a change,
I can be proud of it, in any way.
As long as my heart is filled with joy,
I can pray that I will enjoy.

The difference I can make will start out small,
But then you will see it being recalled.
Making a difference in this world,
is the best way to leave my mark.

My Voice

My voice is a beautiful song,
That has never been sung.
No one else has it because
It was mines to begin with all along.

It is a sound so sweet and pure,
But once you turn around
It is like "boo" you never knew I was here.

The words that come out
It can't be stopped.
The words of wisdom will not be contained,
Not even under your powerful brain.

My voice is my power,
It can not be tamed.
It is important to me,
for it is used to do most things.

Destiny

Destiny is an uncontrollable thing,
It can bring us joy and sorrow.
But it is something we must go through
everyday.

But either way it's there
And we must accept our fate.

We all have a destiny,
Either if it is bad or good.
It all just depends on, well you.

It shapes our lives and paths,
We all have a future,
Somewhere, that is for sure,

Yet what it holds,
A mystery that is yet to be solved.
No one knows where destiny lies.

It is always hard to say.
But the perk of it all,
is how it guides us on our way.

Dream Big

Dream big, make it happen,
Aim for the sky.
Take a chance, make the plan,
Make your dreams come true, if you can.

Create a vision, always strive for success!
Rise up and reach, no need to second guess.
Believe in yourself, you will never be forgotten!

Big dreams ignite your hope,
Visions in and of progress.
There is a wide future ahead,
That can never be dead.

We are high in our hopes that are within our
reach.
Steps taken to give a speech.
Believing in the highest highs
Your dreams will come alive, so wise.

Have faith and courage to succeed.
Embrace the challenge and take the chance you
need,
Your dreams will come true if you just believe,
So dream big and achieve all that is needed.

Progress

Progress is a journey,
A quest to be better,
It shows you what you need to change,
and gives you hope for more.

A shift in the story,
It shows what something could be.
A chance to make things right,
A path to a better life.

There is a vision of the future, so bright.
Look ahead, Evolve, learn, and grow!
Never look back,
Until you know what you can achieve!

Unlock your potential, push up the hill
Progress is the goal!
That you can change,
And make a better future for you and me.

There is a Light

There is always light, a gentle glow
Even in the dark.
It guides us through the darkest days
And revive us in the darkest night.

It shows the path that is ahead,
To make our dreams come true.
It shines on us, a guiding star
The presence of it is near, never too far

It brings joy and comfort,
and brightens our gloom.
Soon it fills us with hope,
showing us where we belong.

Shining within our lives
When darkness falls, it still glows
Illuminating me and you.

The dark can not take away this away,
Making the light the better one everyday.

Balance

Balance is key to life's success,
We don't want too much of one thing,
Or it becomes a disaster all at once.

We must balance work and play,
It is just what life has to say.
Balance helps us stay on track,
so our mistakes don't make an attack.

Balance is hard, but still can be achieved
Knowing it is still there,
will still help you, at least.

Life is a journey of balance,
We search for stability and peace,
A quest to find our purpose in life
A mission to find our worth.

And balance is what is needed in life
To complete what we strive to mend.

Mistakes

My mistake was wrong yet I thought it right.
I felt a sense of guilt and shame,
It was just unlike me, I had not way to fight.

This is a hard lesson to learn
But we can make a turn.
We now know Mistakes are a part of us
And it is okay to make them.

We can instead learn from our errors
And strive to do better.
We can make things right,
If we try with all our might.

Though the mistake was hard to bear
It made me wiser, without a care.

Friends

Friends are like stars in the night,
Shining brightly and giving light.
They are always there for you
Laughing, loving, till day is done.

They always listen with honest care,
Helping others in times of despair.
No matter what, they will be around,
Loving us and keeping us sound.

They lend a helping hand,
Making life less hectic and high.
Holding each other up, until the end.

Through thick and thin, they won't leave.
Forever friends, they will always be!

Teachers

A teacher's job is never done,
they guide us, nurture and inspire,
With the skills and knowledge, they share.
They encourage us and show they care.

They challenge us to think and strive,
And make sure we are alive,
To learn, to explore, and to grow,
Their hard work helps us to know.

They lead us to a brighter future,
Guiding us day and night,
Helping us to make things right,
Giving us the strength to take flight.

Molding us into better souls,
Making us reach our goals,
Showing us the way with their roles,
Inspiring us to be our best selves.

Their hard work is sometimes taken for granted
We should appreciate them before they get
slanted.

The Last Poem for you

And that's how you,
became the person no one else
had the thought to become.
And how she had all the time
just to care about others rather than herself.
She was a social but shy person
who didn't often celebrate her birthday.
People really trusted her,
But she would have many doubts about herself.
But if only someone would get to know her
better before,
it would have mended her broken heart,
And probably let her know that somebody cared
really deeply about her.
You may be remembered
as a lot of things: a student,
maybe a miracle, a good friend,
a successful daughter,
but most importantly,
she should be remembered
as always working to become
the person she always wanted to be.